PERVERSE

A collection of short prose and verse

By Tim Walker

Contents

Introduction

Life is perverse – full of contradictions, disappointments, grief and sheer bloody-mindedness. The proof of all-pervasive perversity is the popularity of narcissistic, morally bankrupt political leaders. There is perversity is the culture of greed, selfishness and corruption that has become the new norm.

I started writing fiction in the aftermath of an almost fatal health crisis in 2012. My slow recovery and time spent indoors led me to take an online creative writing course and start writing short stories. I opted for escapism and chose to write about things I was interested in – history, location, current affairs – and indirectly about myself, thinly disguised in fictional stories.

It's important to mention my health battles and my fears of dying, as this is a strong and recurring theme across this collection of, at times, morose whimsy. But this is balanced by more uplifting content – memories of a happy childhood and reflections on the people I value and love. Resolve and a strong will to survive are also there, and my views of the natural and political world have also been jolted into sharper focus as a consequence of my slow swim towards the light. It's perhaps fitting that I've pulled this collection together whilst self-isolating during the coronavirus crisis of 2020.

For two years I wrote short stories, testing my narrative nerve over a short distance, believing I was making them up. But an analysis of the fifteen stories that now comprise my first book, *Thames Valley Tales* (2015), reveals to me that they are a quixotic memoir, reflecting mood, situation, occupation and interests. The common thread are their settings – places along the course of the River Thames, where I used to live (London) and more recently have lived (Maidenhead, Windsor and Datchet), following my return to England in 2009 after a stint in Africa.

Perverse

I taught myself self-publishing, using the Amazon Kindle Direct Publishing platform. Once bitten by the writing and publishing bug, I embarked on an historical fiction book series – *A Light in the Dark Ages* – that allowed me to indulge my interest in post-Roman Britain. The stories were carefully constructed from bits of information gleaned from research, with the ultimate objective of building a believable (albeit fictional) account of Britain in the Fifth and Sixth centuries that connects the end of Roman occupation to elements of the Arthurian legend.

I joined a local writers' group and continued to write short fiction and the occasional poem. One popular group exercise was to write a 100-word story, a form known as a 'drabble'. Some of my drabbles are included here, together with my poetic ramblings. Most of these poems were written for reciting at spoken word evenings at a local pub – *The Herschel Arms* in Slough – the monthly *Innerverse* nights providing a deadline to spur me into action.

Perverse is my introspective universe - a meld of prose and verse, my twisted version of the *Innerverse*. The role of the writer is to reflect the world as he/she sees and experiences it; and so my fiction and verse reflect my interests, experiences, opinions and the environment I live in. I hope you enjoy this eclectic, quixotic, collection.

Tim Walker, March 2020

www.timwalkerwrites.co.uk

The Middle

Written when I was in secondary school; for some reason it stuck in my memory – the only early poem to have done so.

Then all at once it came to me

A thought of perfect symmetry

I knew exactly where to look

Began to follow like a book

And everything seemed so worthwhile

Essential to my newfound style

Won't have to waste a single day

Now black and white emerge from grey

But where to look and how to say?

What outlet for my thoughts can lay?

In need of a base on which to build

An action plan with notebook filled

With lists, ideas, contacts and dates

Or should I lie back and trust to fate?

Perverse

An obstinate urge or contrary behaviour,

Nurtured in households without a saviour.

Children push boundaries of what is permitted,

Their minders frustrated and often outwitted.

A rebellious nature can lead to conflict,

That soon turns parents into addicts.

To be tasked to set the dining table,

Is not a request that is wholly unreasonable.

But You fold your arms in a stubborn show,

The pout of your lip says, 'no, no, no'.

You say you want to be left alone,

But expect food, shelter and a phone.

Is it an instinct to survive by challenging the norm?

Or a wilful desire to not conform?

A frustrating menace to the rule of law,

Non-conformists' can be such a bore.

Take a bad situation and make it worse,

These are the things that are called 'perverse'.

But before I go, just to be perverse,

I have changed all the fonts in this verse.

Nature Spells Danger!

A remote-controlled trolley moves through the store,
My eagle eye scanning for bargains galore,
Thirst drives me on as I dodge, spin and steer,
Past pasta and peanuts en route to the beer.
My list is all ticked as I join a long queue,
It crawls at a snail's pace; I now need the loo.

My senses are heightened as I move to the car,
Imagining scheming baboons who might steal my jars.
I'm an apex primate with much loot to lose,
As I head to my house in a quiet leafy mews.

A falcon plummets then applies the brakes,
As a young iguana sashays
past some snakes
Whilst Sammy the sloth
swims slowly upstream,
Above cold-eyed pike
hunting plump pink bream.
Are humans above the
circle of life?
Now our primary purpose is
economic strife?

Just stay healthy and
sociable to avoid your doom
Suggests *Living Planet Two*
in my living room.

Trick or Treat?

Samhain, now called Halloween, is a carnival of dread
Groan from an ancient festival when the spirits of the dead
Once more do haunt this earth to terrify all that may
Walk about on this Christian re-branded All Souls Day
Our children dress happily as ghouls and freaks
So they might collect goodies in Trick or Treat
Then stay up late to delay their bed
To watch a film about murderers or the drooling undead
Then in their nightmares dream a Shakespearean dream
Where a churchyard yawns beside a blood red stream
And hell itself breathes out contagion to this world
Where snarling werewolves crouch with claws curled
Whilst above ghosts hover over dancing goblins
Witches throw frogs into boiling cauldrons
Chanting 'Double, double, toil and trouble;
Fire burn and caldron bubble.
Fillet of a fenny snake,
In the caldron boil and bake;
Eye of newt, and toe of frog,
Wool of bat, and tongue of dog,
Adder's fork, and blind-worm's sting,
Lizard's leg, and owlet's wing,
For a charm of powerful trouble,
Like a hell-broth boil and bubble.'
So did the witches in the woods of Dunoon
Conjure a spell that spelt Macbeth's doom
But tremble ye not as you go to your room
And check all the corners in the gathering gloom
That broom didn't move and the cat won't bite
The shimmering curtains in the pale moonlight
All conspire to worry and give you a fright
So, beware of things that go bump in the night
On Halloween you never know it just might
Scare you to death before cold daylight.

Slough, Year 100 AD

We cry and spit the bitter taste of defeat.
Our men slaughtered and our women weep,
Children only remain to harvest the crops.
An ill wind blows along the track to our village,
Ruffling the feathers of a dead owl meant to ward off evil spirits.

We are the Catuvellauni people - fishers of the river, hunters and foragers of the great forest.

When the men from Rome first came, we ran, hid and listened in the gloom to the rhythmic thuds,
clutching our charms to protect us from evil spirits whilst mumbling the words, soon dispelled by the jangle of metal, the tramp of boots, the cries in a foreign tongue.

They enter through a wooden gateway, oblivious to the sacred owl, into our stockade of sharpened stakes
that keep out the animals of the forest and deter other tribes. But not the men from Rome, wherever that may be - A new name for hell, perhaps.

They scattered the fowl and pigs and yapping dogs soon cowered and whimpered.

Their guide tells our headman they will pave our road to make it strong. What is a road? Our grey-haired leader asks.

The narrow tracks that connect our villages have been there since the dawn of time and belong to the gods, given to us by our mother, Brigantia, who whispers to us in the wind.

But now our conquerors will make use of them to keep us at heel. They will connect their forts with these roads of flattened rocks. They are here to stay.

Perverse

Time passes and we have become accustomed to the Romans
They ask for our cooperation from behind a row of red shields,
the sunlight glistening off polished bosses, helmets and spears
Our new masters send men to show us how to grow their crops
- barley, wheat and vegetables we have not seen before.
They take our goats and fowl but give us only round silver discs
This is their money, our elders explain, to barter with at market.
They take our young men and mother's weep,
their tears stain the cracked but unyielding earth,
their cries the anguish of the conquered,
powerless before the new gods of Rome.
Our druid tells us not to be afraid,
But he runs to hide in the forest whenever they approach.
Our young men come to visit and stand proud and tall,
Dressed in the Roman fashion in toga and sandals of leather
We laugh and hug them and covet their shoes.
The Romans have taught them their ways and they understand
their symbols.
They show the boys how to catch fish in nets.
Their laughter entwines with the splash and flash of silver as
they take turns to cast it, small stones dragging it to the depths
where sits Father Tamesis, waiting, giving his bounty.
Our mighty river flows from before the dawn of men -
It feeds and refreshes us and receives our offerings.
Never lying nor betrays, but sometimes takes one of us
We are the new slaves of Rome but one day will be free.
The rushing flow carries our hopes to the sea of life.
They command us but they will never possess our souls.

Down to the Sea

Tiny feet dance on the burning sand
Happily holding Mummy's hand,
Giggling and squinting in the bright white light
White granules reflecting with all their might
A rhythmic lapping of white prancing mares
Whisper a summons to Neptune's wet lair.

I break away from her protection
And run towards the beckoning
big blue,
Her shriek drives me on,
wanting to be chased,
Into the wet unknown,
a brand-new experience with
unknowable consequences.
Onwards into the cool embrace,
giggling, splashing into the sea -
you see it's all just a game to me
She catches me when I'm up to my chest,
Lacking a plan except she knows what's best
Before my mischief leads to whatever I'll find
In my infant's innocent and untested mind.

She lifts me with a cry - relief mixed with rage
Her tight grip tells me it's no longer a game.
It's the end of my adventure now I've been waylaid
Confined to the towel digging holes with my spade.
But I remember the thrill of running into the sea
A defining experience of risk-taker me.

Wood for the Trees

Since the dawn of time a great forest grew
With bushes and trees of beech, oak and yew
Then every year, when the warming begins
They would scatter their seeds in helicopter spins
Or by flowering buds, dropping nuts or seeds
Or enlisting the aid of the birds and the bees
To give the forest a sense of rebirth, in a way
And replace those who had fallen to brown decay
The tree parents would bend and groan in the breeze
Bowing to protect their sprouting saplings
Until one day a stranger did suddenly emerge

With curious swagger and ungainly lurch
Attracting the attention of rabbits and bees
To introduce himself to the curious trees
"I am the axe and I'm just like you
My handle fashioned from the finest yew
I can tell of the outside and many things
If I could play with your fine saplings."
The elder trees moaned and groaned in
the breeze and agreed they would like to
know of these fantastical things that
happened beyond the edge of the trees…
So, they welcomed in the ungainly fellow
And soon the axe had them all enthralled
With tales of people, cars and buildings walled
When the axe saw he had gained their trust
He said, "And now meet my mate, Russ."
Russ jumped among them and picked up his friend
Then began cutting the trees who away did bend
But they could not escape the axe's sharp blade
And soon the sun shone on the unhappy glade.
Soon they stopped to stretch and looked on their mess
Then they put up a sign saying, 'Welcome to Progress'.

Tower Terror

I wake with a jolt as a scream stings my ears,
Was it part of a dream or something to fear?
My settee's like an island that floats on a shroud
Feeling weird my head veers into a hovering cloud
What is happening to my small flat in the skies
On the twentieth floor of a concrete high rise?
The smoke enters my nostrils; I struggle to breathe
I drop down to the carpet on my hands and knees
There's no fire in my flat so it must be the tower
I crawl to the window with diminishing power
Thick black smoke billows up from below
There's no time to waste, it's time to go.

Wriggling on my belly I cross the warm carpet
Coughing and spitting to escape this death pit.
Yes, to escape from danger I came to this place
Somewhere safe to work, a new life to embrace
The crocodile smile of my boss swims before me
Pointing a mop to dirty aisles I can clearly see
This position I'm used to, a place I belong
The invisible worker grovelling all day long
I make the front door and reach for the handle
Outside are flames, the stairwell burns like a candle
There's no one around, I'm here all alone
I pull out my mobile, no signal, I groan.

The smoke makes me dizzy, I roll on the floor
Through the grey thick haze, I see flames lick the door.
My fate is sealed, it's too late to escape,
I crawl back to the window to view a bleak landscape
Blue flashing lights mixed with screams and shouts
I feel weak and lightheaded, there's no bailout.
My family's tear-stained photo I hug as I choke
All my hopes and dreams are going up in smoke.

Northern Lights

Billions of particles
floating through space
Unaware that there might
be a human race
Clusters led by the green aurora
Violet follows like she oughta
Then catching up
comes waves of blue
Alongside a nice
glowing yellow hue
Bringing up the rear
is a bright burning red
On its fringes
a waving purple is led
Particles charged
and sent by the Sun
Penetrate the Earth's
atmosphere one by one
Then dance with delight
in a new found role
As they glow in the skies
above the North Pole

AGAR'S PLOUGH

Morning sunlight shines on dewy grass
Best part of the day to perform my task
I mow the field in stripes thinly shorn
In truth it's better than my own lawn
The pitch has the thinnest layer, almost dust
I paint the white lines as straight as I must
Then drag off my roller as the two teams arrive
Bird song replaced by their banter and jibes.

The sons of Prime Ministers, Dukes and Majors
Communists, Sheiks and third world dictators
Whoever has money in this mad world of ours
Send their sons to Eton where ambition flowers
We fool ourselves that democracy works
But here on this playing field power is learnt
Where tomorrow's leaders their shoulders do rub
Before their induction to the millionaire's club
Regardless of grades or whether they are able
A seat is waiting at the Establishment's table
Where corrupt politicians they can easily clone
And dictate instructions to the media they own.

Perverse

Now the fielding team takes to the field
Stretching and joshing unwilling to yield
The two batsmen emerge swinging their bats
In their college blazers and matching caps
There's Johnson Junior, Morris Minor, Gove and Wynne
An Arabian Prince they call the King of Spin
In truth it matters not who wins this game
On the playing fields of Eton all share in the fame
For a world of privilege is all they will know
Inherited wealth takes them where they will go
The apple of Mother's eye, their father's firstborn son
As far as this game goes, they've already won.

The ball rolls to my feet, I bend to pick it up
Touch my cap as I throw it to a grinning young pup
But my employment is stable, the pay is enough
I smile as I light up, sit back and puff
And think of my Billy and his prospects in Slough
For I am the groundsman at Agar's Plough.

The Enchanted Isle (*ode to WB Yeats*)

I shall arise and go to the enchanted Isle,
Where my mind shall be soothed in quiet reflection,
Through the still waters of the lake, a mirror of the soul;
Ripples spread like pages from my life,
The warmth of the sun on my upturned face,
The freshness of the breeze upon this placid place;
Oarlocks groan to the steady rhythm of my labour,
My guidebook maps out my safe delivery,
I alight and tread the little-worn path,
Passing wild fowl and frogs, birds and bees,
Gnarled oaks randomly bend as thick grass encroaches,
On a procession through nature to the sacred stone.

Its weathered grey face stands at an uneasy angle,
Protruding from the earth where the ancients placed it,
The inscriptions in a long-forgotten hand speak no more
Of the lives of those who have passed;
Whose spirits live on in the wind and the rain
An indelible part of the patchwork landscape
Without remorse, a slight moan of regret,
Their brief lives passed in the blink of an eye
As the seasons change what withers must die
But soon to be replaced by a similar life,
Committed to struggle to stubbornly survive,
On this earth where kindness elicits a smile,
Where we strive to succeed for a very short while.

The gods post warning in thunder so loud
Sun now eclipsed by dark scudding clouds
Waters rises up against my lapping hull,
Hunched progress is painful, slow and dull
Hard, grey horizon blends water and sky,
My impudence punished as I ask 'why?'
But the shore is near and I gratefully land
Looking back to the island, I raise my hand.

16

The Plague

I walked through Corona, though some call it Slough,
Through the wreckage of many lives - I don't know how,
My blood was boiling, a life beyond care,
Eyes bulging as I inhaled the fetid air,
My pulse quickening as my shuffle grew slow,
Passing tumbleweed creepers with nowhere to go,
Past doorway sleepers whose lives forsake pleasure,
Block no one no more, those doors closed forever.
A mangy dog howls and chases its tail,
Side-stepped by droogs and a postman with mail,
I stagger on through gritty, drizzling rain
Ignoring shoe holes and a dull throbbing
pain,
MacDonald's is empty - no one in line,
Beyond, the bright lights of Boots in time,
My empty back pack I stuff with loo roll,
Then pain killers, juices and a soup bowl,
I adjust my mask and make for the till,
Join a queue, keep my distance, pop a pill
Outside I'm cautious, guarding my haul,
Make my way to the bus stop through a
desolate mall,
Then leave the cold drizzle for lightness
and warm,
Lowered mask, ignored stares, embraced
the storm,
I look out the window whilst clutching my
wares,
At the hunch-back shufflers weighed down
by their cares,
Boarded up plots speak of urban decay,
A graveyard for those who fall by the way,
My window steams up and it all becomes vague
As I wonder if I too will succumb to the plague.

The Stars Are Calling

Through the prism of my eye
I watch a busy world flash by
Our planet's riches unfold and delight
As I marvel at nature's power and might
In prayer to the Creator so divine
Give thanks for the wonders that are mine
To gaze on and marvel at all shapes and sizes
The colours of the rainbow in all its guises
Of creatures that crawl, jump and run
All kinds of animals just having fun.

But when I press an eye
to a round glass optic
My telescope takes me to
a world more fantastic
The colourful collage of
life left behind
As I'm drawn to a galaxy
of the mind.
Where distant stars
twinkle a polite 'hello'
And comets pass over a
milky marsh mellow.

Are there far away voices with language unknown?
Do they have cities, planes and phones?
Will Star Men cross space in a momentary blip?
Or will we be the first to make that trip?

So I butter my toast and pour my tea
Watch the actions of men on breakfast TV
I dispense with my chores as I get through the morning
My telescope waits; the stars are calling.

Weetabix Saved Me

The squeak of the trolley
A murmur of voices
Shafts of pale sunlight
The uplifting dawn chorus
I survived another night
The orderly´s smile confirms it
"Weetabix with warm milk?"
My thin body needs it.
My sword is a spoon cutting though it
I lift it to my cracked lips
Savouring the flaky texture
Floating in the milk of human kindness
I chew slowly and swallow.

The nurse appears with my pills
I wash them down with tea
Sink back in the pillow and smile
'You're still here' say drip fed arms
A life extension to see my girl grow
And write about new experiences
And outlive my aging parents
I hope. But that's not for now.
Snores from the next bed
Rattle through his chest.
It's a new day for us all.
I close my eyes
Think of better times
Let my frail body rest,
I'm passing life's test.

Cobwebs of my Mind

Nose pressed against misty window
Bright neon lights flash by
Speeding through the Kingsway tunnel
On our way to New Brighton - to the funfair
Leaving 60s Liverpool behind
The Beatles on the radio, yeah, yeah, yeah
For the screams and excitement of the dodgems.
From the top of the Ferris wheel you can see
the picture postcard Pier Head across the Mersey
Where ships from all over the world
visit the bustling docks and their huge tropical spiders
that crawl out from the banana boats.

I snigger at my sister, candy floss stuck to her face
You can talk she says as I clutch my sticky stick of rock
Everyone's laughing as if the world would never end
My older cousins all had jobs then
They owned a Ford Anglia, the epitome of style
She loves you, yeah, yeah, yeah
We all felt loved then, valued, content
That was before we grew up and the world changed
And turned our city ashen, cold and unsafe
under a shroud of greed and indifference.
Lost innocence replaced by the grime of Gotham
Where desperate people now vote for their abusers
In the vain hope that the abuse will end.

They put a smiley face on it and called it progress.
But through the kaleidoscopic lens of childhood
I remember the real smiles and happy banter
the loving hand on my coat toggles
The woolly hat and mittens,

the grazed knees and cocoa when you got in
And most of all the bright lights of New Brighton
Spinning as if nothing else mattered
Filling the corners of my mind with happy memories
The roots of my journey - a seed bed, a fixing point,
The eternal sprouts of hope,
a fundamental belief in human kindness
the grabbing claw sometimes grasps the white rabbit
That comforts you on the drive home
from darkness into the bright lights of the tunnel of love.

Cherish the Moment

Determined buds push through the snow,

And flower in the warming glow.

Through blooms of parental love and guidance,

I watched you learn to sing and dance.

Holding hands on our cliff edge walk,

You say I never listen when you talk.

I reply that I listen whilst I also think,

The lighthouse appears as the sun starts to sink.

Then tiny black midges do start their attack,

As the gloom settles in on our long walk back.

You told me of wolves; superheroes saving kittens,

You see, my dear, I always do listen.

Whilst I may be going through lists in my head,

You might be wondering when next you'll be fed.

You shock me by saying you'd like to study science,

Where empirical truths shout out their defiance.

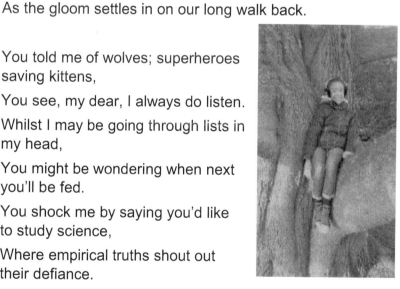

To study human nature and why we're so mean,

And find a new drug to cure the capitalist gene.

It's a matter for science, this climate change thing,

Though we hope common sense will soon spread its wings.

The Ploughman's Hunch

Pinpricks of perspiration he mops with quiet resolve
The unploughed field stretches square and flat
Bounded by hedgerows beneath a calm blue sky
But hungry chorus's strike up in anticipation
From thrushes, sparrows and finches, perched in readiness
He checks his harnessed pair and whispers encouragement
Muscular shires snort and stamp their tasselled hooves
In readiness to drag the plough in parallel lines.
A practiced flick of his reins; they strain against the harness
Birds take to the air and circle noisily above
Their keen eyes fixed on the dark turned earth
The shouts and whistles of the ploughman add to the opera
As birds swoop and squabble over wriggling grey worms
Churned up by steel blades that plough a steady furrow
"Come on my beauties," he urges, and they willingly pull
Up and down the field, until the blade strikes a rock.
"Woah, woah," he commands and they stop.

He walks back to investigate the object,
Shooing birds away with a wave of his arm
Clawing at the precious topsoil with his fingers
Unearthing a dirty lump, he looks in awe
At the head of a Roman emperor on a flat coin
Staring back from across the expanse of time
Telling of wealthy citizens fleeing for their lives
From a murderous warband coming over yonder hill
He stretches his back and swats at a fly
Then puts the grubby coin in his shirt pocket
And once more flicks the reins to set the pair in motion
To plough the field where corn shoots will grow
Between lost coins whose stories lie buried
Beneath the layers of time and human endeavour
Compacting the dark, unforgiving earth
On which our desperate lives unfold
Whilst history beneath our feet remains untold.

Radicalised

Open message: *Hi, I got your name from Ahmed, how are you?*
I'm Fine, <u>who</u> are you?
Call me Mehmet, favoured by the Prophet.
Oh? How does the Prophet favour you?
He has blessed me with a beautiful vision of the future.
You mean the future's so bright, you gotta wear shades???
Do not mock, my friend. A better day is coming for true believers.
I am a believer, and I believe I'm going to university.
Wisdom is good, but our holy book has all the wisdom needed for a good life.
There's no conflict between education and belief in the one true God.
Of course not, my friend, but our minds must remain pure and free.
Look, I don't know where this is going... I'm quite happy with my life. I know who I am.
Allah has guided me to you. I am meeting with our friend, Ahmed, after prayers on Friday. I would like to invite you to join us, just to talk in friendship?
Thanks for the offer but I'm busy revising for my exams. Maybe another time.
The time is now, my friend, for all true believers to come together and be guided to a vision of heaven that can only be found through following the Prophet's teachings. Do not turn away from us.
I'm not turning away, just busy.
What would your friend Ahmed think if you refuse to meet with us? Come for just one hour and see that we are nothing more than friends meeting over a cup of sweet tea. Why not?

Tired eyes guided his troubled mind around the room; posters, maps, photos, awards... his teenage years captured in a collection of objects and pictures.
Well... if it's just a friendly chat, then I guess so. I'll come with Ahmed. See you on Friday.

Chronic Heartache

I inhabit the fringes of life
A wraith gazing mournfully at passers-by,
In a withering haze of pain and torment.
I have no future - only a fretful present,
I have stared into a deep, black abyss
And seen the gaping hole in my troubled soul.
I hug my memories as I pick at my food
My next appointment just more disappointment,
Friends and family ask, 'what's wrong?'
I'm being eaten from the inside out, perhaps
Or mumble, 'I'm fine, just a little tired.'
My disease has a movie face
An alien bursting from a writhing victim.
It's just the way it is
The hand that life deals you,
Slow wasting tinged with fear and regret
On borrowed time, my fate soon will be met.

Timkinson's School Daze

I wake to the stealthy approach of the milk float,
settling silently outside with a squeak of air brakes.
I swing out of bed, my bare feet cold on the thin carpet,
to peer through a curtain crack at the cheery white-
capped fellow rattling bottles and whistling a tuneless
song known only to him.
It's six o'clock and he is illuminated by a street light,
replacing the empties with the full, their cream tops
darker than the white below.
I dress quickly in the chill and go downstairs, the first to
have the day.
Taking the milk from the step to the kitchen, lining them
up inside the fridge door.
Socks the cat purrs her pleasure and curls around my
leg, greedily eying the white bottle I convey to the table.
I fetch a spoon and cereal box, then pour cornflakes in a
bowl.
A sprinkle of sugar and then the creamy top of the milk I
pour, in defiance of Mum's instruction to shake the
bottle.
Only then do I share with the cat.
I mimic my father and turn on the radio,
Rockall, Dogger, Fisher, German Bite.
These magical names I splutter between mouthfuls of
mush as if casting a spell on the North Sea trawlermen.
Soon others join me - my sister and brother in school
uniforms.
They grab their favourite cereals from the cupboard and
their chatter fills the room.
Our mum, the teacher, appears - the steady white flow
keeping my secret as I place my empty bowl in the sink.

Perverse

My sister changes the station to Radio One and pop
music fills the room until mum makes her turn it down.
I don't mind, I've had the shipping forecast.
Today is sport so I return to my room and pack my kit
Into a black canvas drawstring bag.
Slung on my shoulder I leave with a mumbled 'see ya' to
no one in particular and make my way to the bus stop.
My school is the farthest away and so I leave first and
return last, in darkness in the winter months.
My cheeks and ears burn with the cold, but once in the
warmth and light of the double decker I find my friends
and joint in their banter.
Football cards, TV shows, character assassination,
skitting other passenger's or each other's appearance.
We tumble off noisily and jostle our way through the grey
sandstone gates.
I'm near the end of the class roll-call - Smith, Walker,
Wallace, Waterhouse (called 'mouse').
The first of many lists committed to memory through my
shades of grey schooldays.
Boys became awkward, pimply youths, sullen and
resentful, jovial and competitive, not understanding nor
caring of what comes next.

Funnelled like sheep through a
pen; pointed vaguely in the
direction of more learning or the
ominous jobs market.
You must decide or it will be
decided for you.
The inevitability of joining society,
the call of responsibility, the slow
decay of childhood dreams, the boxing of your toys.

DRABBLES...

A drabble is a very short story, up to 100 words. It is a useful devise, common in writing groups, to help develop one's creative writing. Here are some of mine...

Mort de Notre Dame

The hoot of a barn owl was met by the stony glare of a gargoyle, fashioned by medieval masons to guard the holy building from evil. But tonight, they had failed.

A wraith-like figure danced down the aisle, glowing in the cavernous darkness, revenge on her mind.

Orange and yellow flames licked the inside of the monstrous granite cathedral, feeding off rows of wooden pews, torching tapestries and melting lead in stained glass windows that popped colourful shards.

Esmerelda smiled as she skipped barefoot through the barred oak doors, out into the silent square, past the scene of her murder.

The Earth Dies Screaming

"The coral is sick and can't have no babies."

Gerald backed away from the mob, glancing behind at the cliff edge.

"White folks make the sea warm and now Momma is sad," a squat earth-coloured woman growled, fixing Gerald with a look Captain Cook would have recognised.

"But I'm here to help!" he croaked as the dry lip crumbled and he toppled backwards. The islanders looked down impassively as the great green ocean swallowed him.

"Have you seen Professor Brown?" blinked a woman on the path.

A lone gull circled lazily above, its grievous cry hanging in the shimmering haze.

Wish you were here?

The Blade

Arthur transitioned seamlessly from the dull and dusty world of accounts to the quiet of home retirement. Prudence the cat purred her approval, but Maggie was determined to fill his time with trivial domestic tasks that had until then remained happily undone.

"Enter a competition," she had suggested, and so he did.

That was weeks ago, and now he marched steadily behind his Jaguar XV-5 mower. His inch-perfect lines and symmetrical shading would surely deliver the prize.

Mopping his brow at the finish, Arthur glanced behind; then froze at the sight of a solitary, fluttering blade, waving his defeat.

Other Short-ish Stories…

The Waters of Time

"I don't get it," Del said, making no effort to conceal his boredom, "it's just a bath with dangling coloured tubes." He was only two weeks into an enforced work placement.

"Modern art, mate; now pay attention to the punters, not the items," Jeff growled. The grizzled ex-cop had bellied-out with a face-saving job as security guard at a prestigious London gallery following his dismissal from the Met. They floated away from *The Waters of Time*.

Jeff tapped his young colleague on the arm and pointing. A figure in a baseball cap was spraying a slogan across an old master in yellow paint.

"Oy! Come here!" Jeff yelled, as he broke into a waddle. "Del, head him off!"

The youth darted into the modern art gallery, tripped and fell into the iron bath. The two guards converged, and Del, ever clutching his phone, snapped the flailing form as he battled the tubing in his struggle to escape. Jeff looked over Del's shoulder at the picture.

"Nice. Now that's what I call a work of art."

The Shirt

Their cheeks rosy from the biting wind, Annie and Archie wiped the snow from their boots on the kitchen doormat and shut out the cold behind them. A chair was on its side and a broken jar had shed green pasta shells across the red patterned floor tiles.

"Did we do that?" Archie asked, idly crunching the pasta under his sock.

"Of course not," Annie replied, picking up the chair and placing her coat over it. "It must have been Kitty."

"I'm hungry," Archie said, dumping his coat on top of his sister's.

They ambled through to the lounge where mum was standing at the ironing board, her back to them, elbow pressing down hard on a subdued garment. Plumes of steam rose to the ceiling with an angry hiss, creating a curtain of shimmering grey that divided the room. Her hair was standing on end as if she had just rolled out of bed, and the straps of her pinny were dancing in time to the sway of her body, giving her the appearance of a manic orchestra conductor.

Annie approached her and looked up. She gasped at the sight of her mum's bruised cheek and swollen black eye. Mum caught her look and tried to speak, but her voice betrayed her and she croaked like a frog. Archie laughed at the sound, but Annie shot him a reproving glance.

"Oh, my voice!" mum said. "Must be the steam." Dad's white shirt sleeve wiggled as she continued to press hard on the board, the iron gurgling its pleasure.

"What happened to your face, mum?" Annie asked.

32

Perverse

"What? Oh, don't be concerned my dear – I had an accident, that's all."

"Can I have a sandwich?" Archie asked, attempting to touch a round pearl button.

"Hands off dear, that's hot," mum said, standing the iron upright and lifting the shirt by its collar, appraising her handiwork. "I'll make you a sandwich soon. Now run along to your rooms and play. Both of you."

It was an instruction that appealed to Archie who ran out of the room. Annie stood her ground and continued to look up at her mum's battered face.

"What kind of an accident?" she asked.

Mum buttoned the front of the shirt and folded it in a well-practiced drill. "Your father and I had an argument and it got a bit… heated. Nothing to worry about, dear." She attempted to smile, but her cracked lips wobbled and a tear ran down her cheek as she looked down at her daughter.

The steam curtain had lifted and Annie now saw the extent of the messed-up room. The settee was on its back and the sideboard had been swept clean – framed pictures, papers and a shattered vase lay on the carpet beside forlorn daffodils and a water-stained patch. Her roving eye rested on a shoe standing upright on its heel beside the upturned coffee table. She moved to get a better look and gasped in shock at the sight of her father lying on his back, unmoving, with the hilt of a kitchen knife protruding from his chest.

Her mother gripped her shoulders and between sobs mumbled, "Like I said, Annie, it all got a bit heated."

Mr. Popadopalis

He scrunched up the sleeve of his old grey cardi and rubbed the windowpane, creating a grubby porthole through which he peered. His privet hedge was wobbling and he knew why. With a sigh, Mister Popadopalis picked his favourite walking stick from the hall stand and opened the front door. He shuffled slowly along his uneven path; the roots of a neighbour's tree having pushed up the paving slabs at awkward angles to make an unwelcome slalom course.

"Oy! I told you not to put flowers and other stuff into my hedge!" he puffed at an unruly group of a dozen-or-so people.

"'ere 'e is," a middle-aged lump of a woman screeched, her rat's tail hair falling across a blotchy face that glowed with malice. "Come to gloat at our Bobby, 'ave yer?"

"Now look here," the old man said, holding onto his wrought iron gate for support, "I'm the victim here, and this is my house, so clear off!"

A crowd was gathering as others emerged from the twin rows of terraced houses, called 'townhouses' by estate agents.

"You heard him," a burly neighbour said, "stop making a shrine to that scum-bag thief outside his house. That fella got what he deserved, breaking into people's houses in the night."

This precipitated an angry exchange of words between the two factions, with Mister Popadopalis standing uncomfortably between them.

"He killed our Bobby!" a teenaged girl screeched, pointing at the perturbed pensioner.

"He was defending himself and his property," a neighbour replied.

Soon the confrontation became a tussle as residents moved in to dismantle the shrine, throwing bunches of flowers and

34

cards into the gutter. Mister Popadopalis sighed and watched on, reflecting silently on the images that would haunt his remaining nights. He had awoken to the sound of glass breaking and instinctively reached out to the space beside him where his wife had once lain.

He switched on his bedside lamp and noted the time – 2.30 am. Outside the pale glow of a street lamp laid a sliver of light across the carpet where his feet reached for his slippers. He tied his dressing gown belt tightly around his paunch and picked up his rounders bat, moving onto the upstairs landing. He could hear someone treading on broken glass in the passageway that led to the kitchen. His mobile phone was downstairs, most likely on the living room table, so calling the police was not an option.

He had decided not to confront them as they rummaged through his kitchen, and having quietly descended, went to unbolt the front door. The latch made a scraping noise and he heard footsteps behind him. Turning, he saw the silhouette of a taller man, arm raised and holding what appeared to be a knife. In that instant a memory flashed in his mind of him cowering before an assailant during the riots. He brought his arm holding the bat down in the direction of the man's head, connecting with a dull thud that caused the burglar to stagger, swiping a vase off the hall stand and falling heavily, his head bouncing off the solid wooden box that housed a collection of umbrellas and walking sticks. Pulling the door open, Mister Popadopalis scurried down the moonlit path and ran across the road to a friendly neighbour.

"'e ain't even one of us!" the unkempt woman screeched, pointing at the cowering pensioner. "'e's a bleedin' foreigner!" She moved towards the shrinking old man but was intercepted by his neighbour, who slapped the woman across her face. Mister Popadopalis retreated behind his gate as a full-scale fight broke out on the pavement. One female resident was bashing a young man with a bunch of flowers, creating a shower of colourful petals that festooned the mayhem.

"We've got a right to live in peace without the threat of you estate scumbags coming here to rob us!" the female lawyer from two doors down screamed as she kicked the grieving widow, dressed in bulging black leggings under a black hoodie, repeatedly in the ankles.

A siren announced the arrival of a police car and soon two bobbies joined in the brawl.

"What about my 'uman rights and that of my Bobby?" the feisty widow yelled, pulling the blonde lawyer's hair. A policeman stepped between them, grabbing the woman in black by the arm whilst shooting a grin at the lawyer lady.

"We'll let the courts decide, shall we?" he said, dragging the wriggling woman in black to his car.

"Low-life scum," the lawyer lady muttered, brushing down her cream designer jacket and flicking her fringe.

Mister Popadopalis sighed and slowly shuffled back to his porch, passing into what was once a sacred safe space. Closing the door behind him, he glanced up through the multi-

coloured stained-glass window panes at the stormy sky above, a pang of sadness running through him.

He picked up the purring cat coiled around his leg and gazed into her yellow and black eyes. "No matter how many times we call ourselves 'civilised' we'll never escape the deep-rooted tribal instincts lurking beneath the thin veneer of civility that just about prevents us from tearing each other apart. Although at times it inevitably breaks out, like a recurring rash. Time for a nice cup of tea, I think, Mable."

Christmas at the Stones

Stars winked in the deep blue blanket above them as the promise of dawn seeped upwards from the distant edge of the World; a golden glow that prompted the start of the ceremony. Druids holding burning brands chanted to the steady beat of hand drums as a line of riders wrapped in bearskin cloaks watched, their breath trails mingling with those of their horses, rising like the souls of the departed buried beneath, making their way in twisting tendrils to the netherworld.

"Merlin, this had better be the sight you have much talked of," King Uther growled, his horse stamping impatiently on the frozen earth.

"My lord," Merlin replied, "This is the dawn on midwinter day for which these stones were erected and aligned by the ancients who understood the movements of the sun and moon. We are blessed with a clear sight of the rising sun, and you will soon see it shine through yonder stone portal and light up the altar on which a sacrifice will be made to the goddess Beira for seeing us through another winter…"

"My lord!" Bishop Andreus interrupted, causing Uther to turn to his left.

"What is it?" Uther demanded of the shivering, tonsured priest, his white face peeping out from his cowl.

"Beira is a pagan goddess of the druidic religion of the dark forests, banned by our former Roman masters," he said through chattering teeth. "It is not long since the people bowed to the Roman god Saturn at their feast of Saturnalia…"

"And what is your point?" Merlin challenged.

"My point is, the Romans have now departed, taking their gods with them! The older ways of the ancients have passed into legend, banished by the one true Christian God to the dark corners of this land. I urge you to turn away from this base pagan bloodletting and embrace this day as the feast day of the birth of our saviour, Jesus the Christ. For our God is the one true light of the world…"

Uther raised a hand to silence him. "Save the sermon for later, bishop. Now let us bear witness to the mysteries of nature revealed to us."

The smell of incense mixed with sandalwood wafted before them as Merlin pointed, drawing Uther's attention away from the fretting bishop towards the stone altar and the light now bathing it in an eerie glow. Three druids stepped from the shadows, each holding a struggling creature in one hand and a raised knife in the other. Fowls clucked their desperation and kids screamed as their throats were cut and their blood dripped into silver goblets. The drummers increased their tempo as men and women dressed in animal skins and masks danced around the altar where the druids chanted and held their hands up to welcome the rising sun.

"This is an impressive sight," Uther said, grinning his pleasure at Merlin. Bright yellow sunlight was illuminating a hitherto unseen ceremonial avenue bounded by rounded stones from east to west, cutting through the centre of the stone circle.

A golden shaft beamed through the windows of the largest pairs of standing stones on opposing sides of the circle, now in perfect alignment with the rising sun, like a bolt from the gods.

"From this day onwards, our days grow longer," Merlin said, "and hope is restored to the people after the darkness of winter, and the earth is reborn."

"You are forgiven for calling me out on such a cold night," Uther said to Merlin, a broad smile cracking his frozen beard. He turned his horse to signal his readiness to leave and remarked to Bishop Andreus: "And, dear Bishop, we shall pray to the baby Jesus in our church, then progress to our hall where we shall raise a goblet to ALL the gods that they may grant us success in our campaign against the Saxons! Onwards!"

Adapted extract from *Uther's Destiny by Tim Walker*

**Thank you for reading Perverse –
I hope you enjoyed it!**

Please leave a review - a star rating and your impressions.

Tim Walker is the author a children's book series:

- The Adventures of Charly Holmes
- Charly & the Superheroes
- Charly in Space

…and a historical fiction series under the title, *A Light in the Dark Ages*:

- Abandoned
- Ambrosius: Last of the Romans
- Uther's Destiny
- Arthur, *Dux Bellorum*
- Arthur, *Rex Brittonum*

Please visit his website for book news and links, and to sign up for his monthly newsletter:

https://timwalkerwrites.co.uk

Printed in Poland
by Amazon Fulfillment
Poland Sp. z o.o., Wrocław

55804140R00026